Reading FOR CONTENT AND SPEED

Carol Einstein

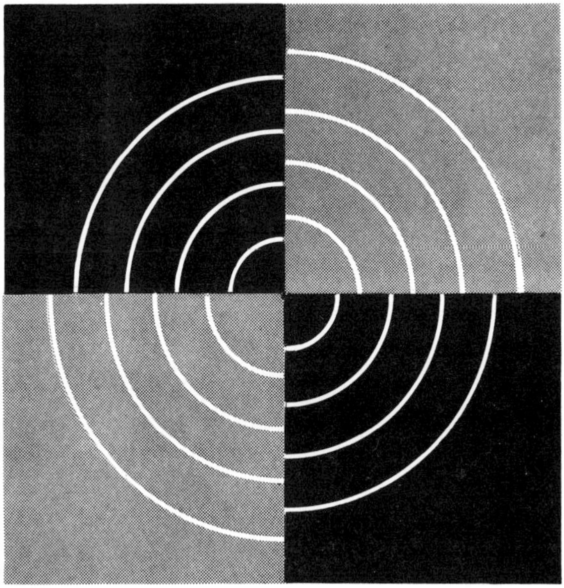

Book 3

EDUCATORS PUBLISHING SERVICE, INC.
75 Moulton Street, Cambridge, Massachusetts 02238

 ISBN 0-8388-1653-3. Printed in U.S.A.

Table of Contents Page

Introduction for the Teacher

Reading for Content and Speed, Book 3, is designed to help improve students' reading speed and comprehension skills. The passages are at a fifth-grade reading level. The readability of the selections is based on classroom testing and on the principles of the Fry Readability Formula.[1] Because of the high interest level of the passages, this book is also designed for use with older students who need remedial assistance.

Four comprehension questions accompany each passage. Questions one and two are main idea questions and questions three and four are conclusion questions. Students circle the letter of the correct answer.

If the book is being used to develop a student's reading speed the student should be given three minutes to read each passage and anwer the four questions. The time limit for the selections is based on data from *How to Increase Reading Ability* by Albert Harris.[2]

Students should be told that if they do not know an answer to a question they should skip it and, if they have time, go back to the question later.

If the book is being used primarily for improving comprehension skills, the student should read the passage and answer the questions in an untimed situation.

The answer sheet and progress graph on pages 88-91 are important aspects of the book. Students can see the types of errors they are making and the teacher can give needed help. Filling in the progress graph in the back allows students to record and chart progress.

---

[1]Edward Fry, "The Readability Principle." *Language Arts* (August 1975), pp. 847-851.

[2]Albert J. Harris and Edward R. Sipay, *How to Increase Reading Ability* (New York: David McKay Co., Inc., 1975).

Directions for Students

For Timed Reading

You will have three minutes to read and answer the four questions on each passage. Follow these steps:

1. Read the passage.
2. Answer the questions. If you are not sure of an answer, skip the question and go to the next question. If you have time, go back and finish the questions that you were having problems with.
3. Correct your answers with the answer key. Plot your comprehension score on the progress graph.

For Untimed Reading

1. Read the passage.
2. Answer the questions. Do all the questions that you know first. Then go back and try to answer the questions that you left out. If you are not sure of an answer it will be helpful to reread the passage to find the answer to the question.
3. Correct your answers with the answer key. Plot your comprehension score on the progress graph.

Passage 1

Roller skating is back and it is booming. People of all ages are skating. They skate outdoors and indoors. Families can enjoy this sport together. They have fun and get good exercise. Roller skates are replacing the more dangerous skate boards.

Makers of roller skates are doing big business. There has been an increase in the number of companies making these skates.

People who can afford them are buying boot-type skates. These may cost from $50 to $250. People who don't want to spend so much money buy the old-fashioned, cheaper, clamp-on skates. These are the skates children have used for so many years.

A new type of wheel is used in today's skates. These wheels have helped to make outdoor skating popular. Plastic wheels are used instead of steel wheels. As a result, skaters enjoy smoother rides. One maker of skates said that these wheels make it possible to skate outdoors "without jarring the eye-teeth out of your head."

The number of roller skating rinks has also been growing steadily. Modern rinks are very different from the old rinks. Some accommodate as many as 3,000 people. Some have air conditioning, special lighting and sound systems, and snack bars.

When allowed, people can also roller skate in parks and on streets. Places and rules for skating vary with each community.

Passage 1

1. What is the biggest expense for a person starting to roller skate?
   a. admission to skating rinks
   b. buying skates
   c. traveling to skating rinks
   d. buying knee pads

2. The most important factor in making outdoor roller skating more enjoyable is
   a. beautiful skating rinks.
   b. a new kind of skate wheel.
   c. comfortable boot-skates.
   d. comfortable skating jackets.

3. We can conclude that people in the roller skating business made the most money
   a. in the 1940s.
   b. in the 1950s.
   c. in the 1960s.
   d. in the 1970s.

4. The main reason that roller skating is becoming more popular than skateboarding is:
   a. It costs less money.
   b. It can be done in rinks and on streets.
   c. It is safer.
   d. It is quicker.

Passage 2

When and where did people start to chew gum? What is chewing gum made of? People in many countries began chewing gum in early times.

For centuries the Greeks have chewed gum made from the bark of the mastic tree. This is a small tree found mainly in Grcccc and Turkey.

Over 1,000 years ago the Mayas, an ancient Indian people who lived in Central and South America, chewed chicle. Chicle comes from the milky juice of the sapodilla tree. This tree grows in tropical rain forests.

The American Indians taught the colonists in New England to chew spruce gum. This gum was made from the resin that forms on the spruce tree when the bark is cut.

In the early 1800s lumps of spruce gum were sold in stores in the eastern part of the United States. Later, people started to chew sweetened paraffin wax.

In the late 1860s chicle was brought here. People liked the gum made with chicle better than that made with spruce and paraffin.

By the early 1900s chewing gum had become very popular. Chewing gum companies made changes. They used new ingredients and flavors. They improved the chewing quality and the taste of gum.

Today the chewing gum industry is a big one. There are about 526 companies in 192 countries. The largest is the Wrigley Company.

Passage 2

1. Modern chewing gum is most closely related to the old
   a. spruce gum.
   b. chicle gum.
   c. paraffin wax gum.
   d. mastic gum.

2. The chewing of gum in the United States began in the
   a. 1400s.
   b. 1600s.
   c. early 1800s.
   d. early 1900s.

3. What is the chief reason for the success of today's chewing gum business?
   a. better colors
   b. more attractive wrappers
   c. better trained workers
   d. more enjoyable flavors

4. We can conclude that chewing gum is bought
   a. worldwide.
   b. mainly by Americans.
   c. chiefly by children.
   d. by more women than men.

Passage 3

Recently a baby dinosaur's nest was found in Montana. This is the first time that such a nest has been found. The skeletons of 15 baby dinosaurs were in a mud nest in a former riverbed. They lived more than 70 million years ago.

The nest is about six feet wide and three feet deep. John Horner, a scientist, had hundreds of the fossil bones moved to a museum. There he was able to put together the skeleton of one baby. He hopes to be able to complete ten more.

The babies seem to have been about one to two months old and about three feet long. The species is unknown. Mr. Horner thinks, though, that it is related to the family of duck-billed dinosaurs. What caused the death of all of these babies is a mystery.

Mr. Horner said, "I tend to think of these animals as behaving somewhat like big ducks." He thinks that they could live on land or in water.

Because their teeth showed wear he thinks that the babies had been chewing. He believes that they were eating some coarse materials or rough water plants from the bottom of the river.

He said, "I kind of have a picture of the mother taking little ones out of the nest to feed for the day and then bringing them back at night."

Passage 3

1. Choose the best answer.
   John Horner put together
   a. one skeleton where he found the bones.
   b. ten skeletons where he found the bones.
   c. one skeleton in a museum.
   d. ten skeletons in a museum.

2. Choose the best answer.
   John Horner was able to find
   a. the exact age and length of the babies.
   b. their exact species.
   c. the cause of their death.
   d. the approximate age and length of the babies.

3. We can conclude that as a scientist John Horner was
   a. careless.
   b. inexperienced.
   c. lazy.
   d. patient.

4. From this passage we can conclude that the baby dinosaurs
   a. had mothers and fathers who cared for them.
   b. had mothers who cared for them.
   c. had nobody to look out for them.
   d. could not leave their nest.

Passage 4

Kentucky Horse Park in Lexington, Kentucky, opened in 1978. This 1,032-acre park is devoted to the horse. It was built as a showplace for all kinds of horses. Visitors see and hear about workhorses as well as thoroughbred horses.

Many special events and contests are held here throughout the year. There is no other place like it.

This park has a cross-country and steeplechase course. There is a half-mile training track and a polo field. There are miles of trails for riding. Visitors may ride around the park in horse-drawn carriages.

Visitors can see a 20-minute color film. The film includes a harness race, horse-show jumping, and a polo match. Horses working in the field and pulling logs are also shown.

One of the buildings is the International Museum of the Horse. Here visitors learn about horses from ancient days to the present time. Photographs, posters, and display cases delight horse-lovers. They can get even more information from a computer.

In a walking tour visitors see how a real horse farm operates. They see horses grazing in pastures. They see them being fed and groomed. They see them getting new shoes. Kentucky Horse Park has the world's longest horse barn.

If there is room, visitors may stay at one of the 263 campsites. However, no reservations can be made.

Passage 4

1. Visitors go to Kentucky Horse Park
   a. in the summer.
   b. in the spring.
   c. in the fall.
   d. throughout the year.

2. Choose the best answer.
   Visitors to Kentucky Horse Park learn about
   a. different types of horses.
   b. prize-winning horses.
   c. workhorses.
   d. circus horses.

3. Choose the best answer.
   We can conclude that Kentucky Horse Park would appeal to
   a. young children.
   b. jockeys.
   c. experienced riders.
   d. all horse lovers.

4. Choose the best answer.
   Parents should take their children to Kentucky Horse Park because they will
   a. get fresh air.
   b. see the countryside.
   c. learn a lot about horses.
   d. enjoy the carriage rides.

Passage 5

In 1978 a 36-year-old American found a Spanish treasure ship that had sunk in 1641.

Burt Webber lived in a small town in Pennsylvania. As a teenager he had dreamed of finding long-lost treasures in sunken ships. He took up scuba diving. He explored stone quarries. He read books about sunken treasures.

For many years, he worked near home for part of the year to support his family. He was a salesman. He also worked in a brick plant. The rest of the year he worked for various treasure expeditions. Unfortunately, these found nothing.

The galleon *Concepción* had smashed into a coral reef southeast of what is now the Dominican Republic. The wooden ship had a huge store of silver and gold in its hold when it sank. Over the years many adventurers had tried in vain to find the ship.

Webber and his search team did much research and preparation before they went looking for this sunken ship. They were able to get bankers to lend them the money they needed. They used scientific instruments and maps made from aerial photographs. They searched for five months with no success.

Then a missing ship's log from the boat was found in England. With this and a new instrument Webber was able to locate the ship. At last they had success!

Passage 5

1. The *Concepción* had a cargo of
   a. coral.
   b. valuable metals.
   c. carved wood.
   d. antique sculptures.

2. Mr. Webber first became interested in treasure-hunting
   a. when he was in high school.
   b. in 1977 when he read a newspaper story about the *Concepción.*
   c. when he read books about sunken treasures to his children.
   d. when he lost his job as a salesman.

3. What was the main reason for Mr. Webber's success?
   a. He was a good scuba diver.
   b. He had a good search team.
   c. He made careful scientific preparations.
   d. He had a lot of money.

4. We can conclude that Mr. Webber was a
   a. man with no interest in his family.
   b. foolish dreamer.
   c. lazy man.
   d. man who did not give up easily.

Passage 6

Galileo Galilei was a great scientist.

He was born in Italy in 1564. One day, when he was 17, he was in a cathedral. It is said that he saw a great lamp hanging from the roof. He noticed that regardless of distance its swings always seemed to take the same amount of time. At home Galileo did experiments to try to prove his observation. He found that he was right.

He was the first scientist to rely chiefly on his own experiments to prove a theory. This was a new way for scientists to work.

Galileo also built the first telescope that could be used to study the heavens. With it he made the first map of the moon. He found that the moon's surface was rough. He saw spots on the sun. He also saw that the Milky Way was made up of a group of stars.

During Galileo's time people thought that the earth was the center of the universe. Galileo, though, thought that the earth went around the sun. His discoveries helped prove that the earth was not the center of the universe. He wrote a book about his work. People became interested in his ideas.

However, a powerful court called the Inquisition disagreed with Galileo. Because of his theories about the universe the Inquisition sentenced him to house arrest for the rest of his life. He died eight years later at the age of 78.

Passage 6

1. Choose the best answer.
   Galileo can be called the first modern scientist because he
   a. was so well-educated.
   b. used advanced equipment.
   c. experimented to test his theories.
   d. wrote books about his work.

2. Galileo was a pioneer in the field of
   a. astronomy.
   b. biology.
   c. chemistry.
   d. geology.

3. People might describe Galileo as being
   a. very curious.
   b. popular.
   c. wealthy.
   d. fearful.

4. We can conclude that during Galileo's time
   a. everyone was interested in exploring the moon.
   b. most people did their own experiments.
   c. new ideas could be dangerous.
   d. inventors were free to do as they pleased.

Passage 7

Potato chips were invented in 1853 in Saratoga Springs, New York.

One day Cornelius Vanderbilt, a well-known millionaire, was eating at a restaurant in Saratoga Springs. He sent his French fried potatoes back to the kitchen. He said that they were too thick. The angry chef, George Crumbs, then sliced the new order of potatoes paper-thin. He fried them in boiling oil. When they were served, Mr. Vanderbilt, much to the chef's surprise, loved them. Soon Saratoga chips, as they were then called, were a favorite there.

Saratoga Springs was a famous vacation resort. People from all over the country came there. When they returned to their homes they talked about the delicious new food they had eaten. Soon chips were sold all over the country.

Making chips became a new business. People didn't need much money to start this business. They could work in their own kitchens. All they needed was a large kettle, cooking oil, salt, and potatoes. When the chips were done, they were sent to neighborhood stores. They were sold in small brown paper bags. Sometimes people called chippers went through towns on bikes. They sold chips as they rode along.

Many of the major potato chip companies started as small home businesses.

Today there are about 200 potato chip companies in the United States. The average American eats about four pounds of potato chips a year.

Passage 7

1. Potato chips were invented
   a. after much research.
   b. by accident.
   c. by a large company.
   d. by many chefs working together.

2. The potato chip business grew because
   a. chips were easy to produce.
   b. chips were a healthy food.
   c. people wanted to copy Mr. Vanderbilt.
   d. chips had so much publicity.

3. We can conclude that Mr. Vanderbilt was
   a. fussy about his food.
   b. easy to please.
   c. liked by the restaurant chef.
   d. on a strict diet.

4. We can conclude that in the 1880s potato chips
   a. were expensive.
   b. were quite cheap.
   c. never became stale.
   d. were shipped across the nation.

Passage 8

Mary Cassatt is considered America's most famous woman artist.

She was born in Pennsylvania in 1844. When she was a child Mary and her family spent five years traveling and living in Europe. Mary saw the great art museums. She was determined to become an artist.

When she was 17 she said that she wanted to go to Paris to study art. At that time people thought that only men could become painters. It was not considered proper work for a woman. Her father refused to let her study art. Finally he said she could study it if she went to a school near their home. She attended the Pennsylvania Academy of Fine Arts.

At her graduation in 1866 she again said that she had to go abroad to learn more about painting. Her father agreed to let her go. At 22 she sailed for Paris. She lived in France, but she went to other countries in Europe. She spent time in museums.

She worked hard to improve her work. She studied the famous paintings of the old masters. She copied and sketched for hours.

She found, though, that she preferred the new ideas and techniques used by a group of artists living in Paris. They called themselves impressionists. Like them Mary Cassatt tried to show real people and the real world. Because these ideas were new it took some years before people recognized her as the great artist she was.

Passage 8

1. Mary Cassatt went to art school near home because
   a. she did not have enough money to go away.
   b. she was frightened about leaving home.
   c. her father would not let her leave home.
   d. it was the best school.

2. Mary Cassatt showed that she was serious about becoming an artist by
   a. spending long hours painting.
   b. taking many trips to Europe.
   c. reading many art books.
   d. talking to older artists.

3. From this passage we can conclude that in the 1800s
   a. all careers were open to women.
   b. some careers were not open to women.
   c. all women wanted to stay at home and have children.
   d. men artists welcomed women artists.

4. We can conclude that Mary Cassatt became a great artist because she
   a. came from a rich family.
   b. had great talent.
   c. had good teachers.
   d. traveled in Europe.

Passage 9

The only elephant orphanage in the world is in Sri Lanka, an island nation south of India.

There elephants are highly valued. They are prized for both religious and practical reasons. They are closely connected with Buddha, the founder of the Buddhist faith. The lumber business uses them to move logs to places where machines can't go.

In the past 30 years the number of elephants has decreased from 5,000 to 2,000. There are a few reasons for this. Some have died in accidents. Sri Lanka has many gem pits. When babies become separated from their parents, they sometimes fall into one of them.

Often elephants are wounded when they step on spiked barriers put up by villagers. If their wounds become infected, they can die. They can also die from gunshot wounds. Although it is against the law, people try to shoot them.

As rural sections develop, elephants lose much of their natural homeland. They have no place to go.

In order to stop the elephant decline Sri Lanka set up a 42-acre orphanage. Not all elephants can be cared for there. Some are given as gifts to Buddhist temples. Others are given to foreign zoos. For example, in 1976 one was given to the National Zoo in Washington as a bicentennial gift. The government has also built elephant sanctuaries in national parks.

Passage 9

1. Choose the best title.
   a. Sri Lanka, an Island Nation
   b. The Importance of Elephants
   c. Elephants in Sri Lanka
   d. The Decline of the Elephant Population

2. In Sri Lanka elephants are highly thought of because
   a. their hides sell for high prices.
   b. they help in transportation.
   c. they are used for work in gem pits.
   d. circus owners pay a lot for them.

3. In ten years how many elephants will there be in Sri Lanka?
   a. 5,000
   b. 4,000
   c. 2,000
   d. none

4. Within the next few years Sri Lanka will
   a. have fences around their gem pits.
   b. have fewer elephant sanctuaries.
   c. have more spiked barriers.
   d. allow people to shoot elephants.

Passage 10

The World Trade Center brings together in one place about 900 government agencies and private firms involved in foreign trade. It is on a 16-acre site in lower Manhattan. The Center is near the Hudson River. That is where New York City began.

The Center's twin towers and four low-rise buildings are on an open plaza. This plaza is the size of four football fields. The two 110-story towers are 1,350 feet high. They are the tallest buildings in New York. They have 43,600 windows.

The World Trade Center was completed in 1977. It was built by the states of New York and New Jersey. They thought it would improve the New York-New Jersey port. They believed it would also improve American import-export trade.

The elevators in the twin towers run like trains in a transit system. Express and local elevators whisk people to the floors to which they want to go. There are lobbies on the ground, the 44th, and the 78th floors. On these floors people can change from express to local elevators. If they wish to go directly to the 107th floor with no stops, they can take the express cars.

From an open rooftop promenade above the 110th floor visitors have a sweeping view of the New York-New Jersey harbor. This is the world's highest outdoor observation platform.

There are 30 restaurants in the World Trade Center. They offer many different kinds of food at varied prices.

Passage 10

1. The World Trade Center was built to improve
   a. the restaurant business.
   b. the tourist industry.
   c. foreign trade.
   d. the hotel business.

2. The World Trade Center consists of
   a. six of the tallest buildings in New York.
   b. twin towers.
   c. twin towers and four buildings lower in height.
   d. four buildings of the same height.

3. We can conclude that most visitors to the World Trade Center
   a. are afraid to eat at the restaurants on the highest floors.
   b. will have to leave the Center to eat.
   c. must wait a long time to get to the restaurants on the upper floors.
   d. will find restaurants they will like.

4. Choose the best answer.
   Most tourists go to the World Trade Center because they want to
   a. eat at a good restaurant.
   b. see the view from the observation deck.
   c. see the art that decorates the plaza.
   d. walk around lower Manhattan.

Passage 11

In 1922 Howard Carter, a British archaeologist, discovered the tomb of Tutankhamen. Tutankhamen, also known as King Tut, was an ancient Egyptian king who died at the age of 18 or 19. Carter spent 15 years searching for his tomb.

Carter thought that there must be undiscovered tombs in ancient Egypt's royal burial ground. He was sure that a small part of it had not been searched. Most people disagreed.

A few days after his crew started digging they found the beginning of a staircase. It seemed like the entrance to a tomb. When the staircase was cleared they saw the top of a doorway. Carter's search was paid for by Lord Carnarvon, a wealthy Englishman. Carter wired Carnarvon about his discovery.

When Carnarvon arrived Carter drilled a small hole through the door. The glint of gold could be seen everywhere. Weapons, vases, and chariots were strewn about. The tomb had been broken into. Carter thought it had been robbed twice, probably soon after the burial.

A few months later the Burial Chamber of the tomb could be entered. King Tut's body was enclosed in three coffins. The inner coffin was solid gold. When it was opened they saw King Tut's head and shoulders covered with a fabulous gold funeral mask. Attached to the body and its wrappings were 143 jewels and amulets.

Carter and his staff worked 10 years to clean and preserve the treasures of this four-room tomb.

Passage 11

1. Choose the best title.
   a. Tombs of Ancient Egypt
   b. An Ancient Egyptian King's Tomb
   c. The Work of an American Archaeologist
   d. Ancient Burial Grounds

2. King Tut's tomb was robbed
   a. just before Carter discovered it.
   b. thousands of years ago.
   c. 100 years ago.
   d. in 1922.

3. We can conclude that Carter was a man who
   a. had great wealth.
   b. did not give up easily.
   c. had no patience.
   d. had no imagination.

4. Who would be least interested in the discovery of King Tut's tomb?
   a. historians
   b. jewelers
   c. scientists
   d. athletes

Passage 12

Thomas Jefferson loved his home in Virginia.

As a boy he had dreamed of building a house on a mountaintop. In 1760, when he was 17, he found a beautiful hill. Later, he was able to buy that land.

Thomas Jefferson drew the plans for his house himself. He designed and built a great house with beautiful gardens and parks. The house was called Monticello, which in Italian means little mountain.

Building the house was difficult. Trees had to be cut and made into lumber. Bricks were made from raw clay. Even the nails had to be handmade. He taught people how to do these jobs.

Jefferson was so interested in his house that he even designed the furniture. He invented many useful gadgets. One of these was a fold-up bed. When the bed wasn't being used, it was raised to the ceiling by ropes. He invented a small elevator or dumbwaiter which helped him get his food quickly. Jefferson also built a compass on the living room ceiling. He connected it to the weather vane on the roof. Then he could always tell the wind direction.

Jefferson tried new ideas outdoors, too. He used new planting methods to improve the soil. He imported melons and new types of nut trees. Sheep were also imported to improve his own breed.

Today his home is open to the public. All who go there marvel at Thomas Jefferson's great inventiveness and ability to carry out his ideas.

Passage 12

1. Choose the best title.
   a. The Life of Thomas Jefferson
   b. The History of Virginia
   c. Thomas Jefferson's Monticello
   d. An American Monument

2. Choose the best answer.
   Jefferson's imagination is seen in
   a. all of Monticello.
   b. the garden at Monticello.
   c. the farm at Monticello.
   d. the house at Monticello.

3. Jefferson's inventions show us that he was
   a. a practical man.
   b. not always practical.
   c. interested only in improving his house.
   d. interested only in science.

4. After visiting Monticello most people would conclude that Jefferson
   a. did not follow through on his ideas.
   b. did not help his workmen.
   c. was ahead of his time.
   d. wasted his land.

Passage 13

Building and furnishing doll houses is a hobby popular with people of all ages.

In 1978 a 16-room doll house called Titania's Palace was sold in London for $256,500. Sir Neville Wilkinson started this doll house in 1907 for his three-year old daughter. He finished it 15 years later. It is one of the most elaborate doll houses ever built.

For many years it was shown all over the world to raise money for charity. People are fascinated by this richly furnished doll house.

It is large. The length is 116 inches. The width is 90 inches. The height is about 30 inches. It is mounted on a waist-high platform. All rooms have electric lights. On the walls are miniature paintings made by famous artists.

In the entrance hall water comes out of a gold faucet inlaid with diamonds. A silver door leads to a chapel with stained glass windows and a marble floor. In the chapel there is a working organ.

One of the rooms is a throne room. The throne is made of ebony and ivory. It is decorated with gold figures and birds set with precious jewels.

In a child's room there is a gold bicycle with wheels set with sapphires. The Jack-in-the-boxes are made of gold and silver.

Titania's room has a dressing table with tiny brushes, combs, and a boot hook. Her work table has tiny paint brushes and a palette.

Passage 13

1. According to this passage many of the furnishings of Titania's Palace were made of
   a. beautiful silk.
   b. expensive wood.
   c. precious metals and jewels.
   d. fine marble.

2. According to this passage this doll house
   a. is smaller than most well-known doll houses.
   b. is larger than most well-known doll houses.
   c. was completed in a short time.
   d. was completed in the 1930's.

3. We can conclude that doll house collecting is popular in
   a. the United States.
   b. England.
   c. France.
   d. many countries.

4. Neville Wilkinson was able to build Titania's Palace because he was
   a. a smart man.
   b. a rich man.
   c. an artist.
   d. a good father.

Passage 14

The best known baseball bat is the "Louisville Slugger." It is made by Hillerich and Bradsby. This is the oldest and largest bat-making firm in the world.

The story of the "Slugger" goes back to 1884. In that year Pete Browning was the star of the Louisville, Kentucky baseball team. One day Pete broke his best bat in a game.

Bud Hillerich was an 18-year old fan. He offered to make Pete Browning a bat in his father's wood turning shop. He used a piece of ash. The next day Pete used the bat. He got three out of three hits. Soon other players were coming to Bud Hillerich for their bats.

Bud registered the trademark for his "Louisville Slugger." In 1905 Honus Wagner, a famous ballplayer, signed a contract with Bud's firm. Honus agreed to have his signature on the "Slugger." This was the first time that a player's signature appeared on a bat.

Ash is still used to make the "Slugger." The wood's weight, strength, and moisture content make this bat very powerful. Now an aluminum model is also made.

"Slugger" bats may have famous players' names on them. However, these bats are not always the same models used by the players. Because young people can't handle the heavy bats built for major league players their bats are lighter.

Professional bats are very expensive. The "Slugger" models that are sold in stores are cheaper than those used by professionals.

Passage 14

1. Bud Hillerich made a good bat after
   a. he had tried many different woods.
   b. Pete told him what to do.
   c. he had worked on it for many years.
   d. he had worked on it for a short time.

2. Ash is used to make the "Slugger" because it is
   a. cheap.
   b. plentiful.
   c. strong.
   d. attractive.

3. We can conclude that Bud Hillerich
   a. was wealthy when he started his business.
   b. was an unhappy person.
   c. was a good baseball player.
   d. believed in advertising.

4. From this passage we can conclude that Bud Hillerich's first success in the bat business was due to
   a. his fine tools.
   b. his hard work.
   c. his father's help.
   d. Pete's fine hitting.

Passage 15

Men, women, and children are scuba diving. It is not recommended, though, for young children. Scuba diving first became popular in the mid-1950s. Interest in it is growing now.

A scuba is a machine divers carry. It allows them to breathe underwater. Divers carry a lot of other equipment, too. They wear wet suits, life jackets, scuba masks, and fins. They have knives attached to their belts. They wear watches and depth gauges, too. The depth gauge measures how far down they go. Learning how to use this equipment is a 'must' for safety.

Before starting this sport one should have a check-up. Physical fitness is important. A course of lectures and practice in scuba diving given by experts are needed, too. This training can cost a lot, but some "Y's" give cheaper courses.

Without good training one could panic in a dangerous situation. Divers should know what happens to the body underwater. They should always dive with a partner. They should know signals to use to keep in touch with the partner. These are important safety measures. Sea animals can be a danger. Divers fear sharks and moray eels.

Because there are so many pleasures in scuba diving people do not think of the risks. They find the plunge thrilling. Camera fans delight in great underwater shots.

Scuba fans dream of distant places like the Bahamas. If they can't go that far, though, they can go to nearer spots. Nature lovers find scuba diving beautiful and exciting as they learn about underwater life.

Passage 15

1. Scuba diving is a sport that
   a. can be done without any special training.
   b. requires special training.
   c. requires no swimming ability.
   d. helps develop the body.

2. Choose the best answer.
   Scuba diving has become popular because it is
   a. safe for everyone.
   b. an exciting sport.
   c. good for one's health.
   d. the "thing to do."

3. This passage suggests that scuba diving
   a. can be an expensive sport.
   b. should be practiced alone.
   c. requires no special equipment.
   d. requires no special skills.

4. Choose the best answer.
   We can conclude that scuba diving has helped bring tourists to
   a. Florida.
   b. the Swiss Alps.
   c. the Middle West.
   d. New York State.

Passage 16

Plato, an ancient Greek philosopher and writer, told in his books of a rich island called Atlantis. About 20 million people lived on it. From 12,000 to 9,000 B.C., the people of Atlantis ruled a great empire. They tried to conquer the whole world, but they were defeated by the Greeks.

After the Greeks entered Atlantis there were great earthquakes and floods. In one day and night Atlantis was swallowed up by the sea. Many people have tried to find this lost island. Thousands of books and stories have been written about it.

A well-known book is the one written by Otto Muck, an Austrian engineer. It was published in 1976. He thought that Atlantis could be found near the Azores. This is a group of islands in the Atlantic Ocean.

When experts went there they studied the ocean's floor. They found a large plateau. Its size and shape were very much like Plato's description of Atlantis. They concluded that this plateau was Atlantis.

Mr. Muck thought that a falling asteroid had destroyed Atlantis. When it entered the earth's atmosphere the asteroid blew up. Then it dropped through the earth's crust. Volcanic reactions were set off. The island of Atlantis sank. The nine lava-covered mountain tops which were left above the water are called the Azores.

According to Mr. Muck, this asteroid destroyed much of the world. When the world finally recovered, Atlantis was only a name.

Passage 16

1. A good title for this passage is
   a. Otto Muck's Life
   b. Plato, An Ancient Greek Writer
   c. A Great Mediterranean Empire
   d. The Story of Atlantis

2. Mr. Muck believed that Atlantis had been destroyed by
   a. a great flood.
   b. an earthquake.
   c. a falling star.
   d. an asteroid.

3. People remember Atlantis because
   a. the Greeks defeated it.
   b. it was a wealthy island.
   c. it disappeared in a strange way.
   d. it had an interesting culture.

4. From this passage we can conclude that
   a. a great nation can be destroyed quickly.
   b. a great nation can't be destroyed.
   c. great nations can always control nature.
   d. the Greeks were stronger than nature.

Passage 17

Do you live in a place where the winters are cold? Do you like outdoor winter sports? If so, you probably would appreciate some tips on how to stay warm.

You should learn how to retain your body's heat. When dressing, do not rely only on the thermometer. It does not tell the whole story about how cold the weather is outside.

The speed of the wind is important. Wind or moving air reduces body heat. This is called the wind-chill factor. TV and radio weather broadcasters tell about the wind-chill factor when they announce weather conditions. For example, they may say "The temperature is 34 degrees, but with the wind-chill factor it feels like 10 degrees."

When dressing in cold weather, wear several layers of light clothing instead of just one heavy garment. A few light sweaters are better than one heavy one.

Try to avoid getting your skin and clothing wet. Your body loses heat when it gets wet. Hands and feet lose body heat quickly. Keep them as warm and as dry as possible. You might need two pairs of socks and a pair of gloves under a pair of mittens. Wear waterproof shoes or boots.

A high percentage of the heat you lose when you go outdoors in winter comes from an uncovered head. Be sure to wear a hat or scarf that protects your head.

If you have to stay out in the cold, try to exercise. Exercise increases the body heat.

Passage 17

1. When dressing for the cold weather, it is best to wear a
   a. very heavy, waterproof coat.
   b. heavy, warm coat and a heavy sweater.
   c. warm coat, a light sweater, gloves, and a hat.
   d. warm coat, a light sweater, gloves, a hat, and waterproof boots.

2. To help retain your body heat in winter you should wear
   a. bright-colored clothes.
   b. comfortable shoes.
   c. a hat.
   d. blue jeans.

3. Knowing how to protect oneself against the cold is most important for a person living in
   a. California.
   b. Florida.
   c. North Dakota.
   d. Georgia.

4. Before leaving for school on a cold, snowy winter morning it would be best to
   a. read the outside thermometer.
   b. look out of the window.
   c. listen to the weather reports on the radio.
   d. telephone the school.

Passage 18

The first seeing-eye dog came to this country in 1928.

In 1927 Frank Morris, a blind man in Tennessee, had an article read to him about seeing-eye dogs in Germany. The author, Dorothy Eustis, was a rich dog breeder in Switzerland. She told how soldiers blinded in World War I had learned to use German shepherds as guide dogs. The dogs wore a special U-shaped harness. This made it possible for master and dog to communicate. These dogs helped the men lead independent lives.

Frank Morris wrote Mrs. Eustis to ask if she could get him a guide dog. Mrs. Eustis agreed. He spent a month at her home. Her dog trainer taught him how to communicate with his dog Buddy through a harness. Morris learned that Buddy worked because he loved his master and wanted to please him. He learned that love and praise meant a lot to Buddy.

When Morris came home with Buddy he gave many talks and demonstrations. People learned that guide dogs can help blind people lead full lives. Many blind people asked how they could get these dogs.

In 1929 Frank Morris and Dorothy Eustis opened The Seeing Eye in Nashville, Tennessee. This school trained blind people to use guide dogs. Later the school moved to Morristown, New Jersey.

The Seeing Eye still uses shepherds. However, Labradors, golden retrievers, and mixed breeds are also used. The dogs are usually females. Females are used because they are smaller and easier to manage.

Today other agencies also supply guide dogs to the blind.

Passage 18

1. Where were seeing eye dogs first used?
   a. in Germany
   b. in the United States
   c. in Switzerland
   d. in France

2. The Seeing Eye uses
   a. only purebred dogs.
   b. only one breed of dogs.
   c. all breeds of dogs.
   d. mostly female dogs.

3. In addition to a guide dog, what is most important to a blind person?
   a. a cane.
   b. a harness.
   c. a leash.
   d. a sighted friend.

4. Choose the best answer.
   We can conclude that Frank Morris
   a. was afraid to take chances.
   b. loved to travel.
   c. wanted to lead an independent life.
   d. loved dogs.

Passage 19

Today many young Americans want to know more about their families. They want to find out about their ancestors. They want to investigate the past. They want to learn who their relatives were, where they lived, and what they did. They are curious about their family history. They are searching for their roots.

The United States is a nation of immigrants. People came here from all over the world. Many tried to forget their past. They thought that if they learned the customs of their new country they would fit in and would not seem to be foreigners.

Some groups did continue to practice their native customs. They were proud of their backgrounds. They talked of their families and homes in "the old country." People with such relatives find it easier to trace their roots. The search is not so hard. They already know some family history from grandparents or great-grandparents.

How can descendants of immigrants find out about their roots? They should begin by questioning all older relatives. They should write to people in the towns their family came from, here and abroad. If possible, they should make trips to these places.

When they get there, searchers should go over old church, court, and census records. They should ask local librarians for help. They should question town or city officials. They should talk to older people still living in these places. They should visit the cemeteries.

To get information one must keep searching. One must be a real detective!

Passage 19

1. Choose the best answer.
   People are searching for their roots because
   a. they think they may inherit money.
   b. it is a popular thing to do.
   c. they want to learn about their family history.
   d. they want to travel.

2. The search for roots should begin
   a. in foreign countries.
   b. at home.
   c. in libraries.
   d. by checking church lists.

3. Learning about one's roots is
   a. always easy.
   b. easier if relatives can help.
   c. rarely successful.
   d. successful only if one can travel abroad.

4. Choose the best answer.
   To succeed in finding one's roots a person must
   a. be old.
   b. be rich.
   c. be clever.
   d. use all clues.

Passage 20

Marie Curie, who died in 1934, is the most famous of all women scientists. She was born in Poland in 1867. She was the youngest child in a poor, but closely knit family. Her father was a high school teacher.

When Marie was 18, she left home to work as a governess. She needed money to help her elder sister, Bronya, go to Paris. Bronya went there to study to be a doctor. A few years later she helped Marie come to Paris.

What Marie wanted most was to study math and physics at the Sorbonne, the great French university. She was the only woman in her physics class. As a student she had little money. She almost starved to death. She was first in her class when she graduated in 1893.

In 1895 she married Pierre Curie, a French physicist. The Curies had a happy home with their two little girls. Pierre and Marie spent most of their time working together doing research in their laboratory. Their greatest discovery was radium. Radium is used in science and medicine. It is used to treat cancer.

Pierre was killed in a street accident in 1906. Marie was asked to take his place as a professor at the Sorbonne. She was the first woman professor at the Sorbonne.

For the rest of her life Marie continued her research in physics and chemistry. Many honors came to her from all over the world. She did not want fame, though. She wanted to spend her time in the laboratory, making new discoveries in science.

Passage 20

1. Marie used the money she made as a governess to
   a. go to Paris to study.
   b. help her sister go to Paris to study.
   c. support her father.
   d. buy books.

2. Being a student in Paris was hard for Marie because
   a. she was too poor to buy enough food.
   b. the classes were too difficult for her.
   c. she was often lonely.
   d. she could not take much time off.

3. We can conclude that Marie Curie became a famous scientist because she
   a. studied at the Sorbonne.
   b. was married to a famous scientist.
   c. was a woman.
   d. made some important discoveries.

4. The Curies' happy marriage was probably due to the fact that they
   a. were both French.
   b. had two children.
   c. were both interested in science.
   d. both loved music and the theater.

Passage 21

The sun is our greatest source of energy. We have started to use this energy only recently, though.

The sun can heat houses. Solar heat can keep a house warm even when it is cold outside. Sunny windows, sunrooms, and solar greenhouses all collect the sun's heat. They are solar collectors. They can be made on a roof, a wall, or anywhere the sun shines. Collectors can be made to store extra heat for times when there is no sun.

The sun heats water, too. Pipe systems are put on roofs and the sun heats the water pipes. House roofs should slant toward the south.

In a house that is built especially for solar heat most of the rooms face south. The southern wall has double panes of glass. The panes are divided by a half-inch of space. This space reduces the amount of heat that escapes. The sun can still enter, though.

Solar energy can be used for cooking, too. Dr. Maria Telkes invented a simple stove that looks like a tightly insulated box. The stove tilts toward the sun. Four flat mirrors fan out from it. These mirrors reflect sunlight into the inside of the stove, which is filled with a heat-absorbent salt. Its temperature can be regulated by moving the mirrors. Because it stores up heat the stove can be used after sunset.

Solar energy is expected to become cheaper and more common. Then it will be able to compete with oil and gas as a major source of energy.

Passage 21

1. Choose the best title.
   a. Comparing Different Types of Energy
   b. Cooking With Solar Energy
   c. How Solar Energy Works
   d. Solar Energy, Today and Tomorrow

2. One can identify a solar home by its
   a. construction.
   b. size.
   c. special coloring.
   d. cost.

3. Who would not welcome the growth of solar energy?
   a. air pollution agencies
   b. oil companies
   c. homeowners
   d. construction companies

4. Who would benefit most from using Dr. Telkes's stove?
   a. wealthy people who live in rainy areas
   b. wealthy people who live in sunny areas
   c. poor people who live in cloudy areas
   d. poor people who live in sunny areas

Passage 22

Vince Lombardi was a great football coach.

In 1959 he became coach of the Green Bay Packers, a losing team. When the Packers asked him to be head coach Lombardi was delighted. He wanted to build his own winning team. By the end of the year the Packers had a winning record.

He was the Green Bay coach for nine years. During this time his team won five National League championships and two Super Bowls. Vince Lombardi developed the team by constant drill and by teaching his Lombardi System. This system stressed running. It also taught the players to control the ball on the ground. Because it encouraged strong team spirit players were able to work together to change their playing style.

He first coached football at a New Jersey high school. His team became winners. Although he praised his players he lost his temper too often.

His first college football coaching job was at Fordham. He was the freshman coach there for two years. Then he went to West Point, where he was an assistant to the coach, Colonel Blaik. Colonel Blaik taught him the importance of devotion, discipline, and planning in football. There Vince Lombardi also learned to control his temper. Later he became an assistant offense coach for the New York Giants. He soon built a strong offense.

After his long career as a winning coach Vince Lombardi decided to retire. He missed coaching, though. He went back to work. He became coach and part owner of the losing Washington Redskins. The team soon improved. A year later, in 1970, he became ill and died.

Passage 22

1. Vince Lombardi was respected as a coach because he
   a. was gentle and understanding.
   b. stressed fair play.
   c. stressed the passing game.
   d. developed winning teams.

2. Lombardi's team was able to learn new plays because they
   a. were all great players.
   b. cooperated with one another.
   c. feared Vince.
   d. liked Vince.

3. We can conclude that Vince Lombardi learned most about coaching from working
   a. at Fordham.
   b. at West Point.
   c. with the New York Giants.
   d. with the Green Bay Packers.

4. Which of these teams would Vince Lombardi have least liked to coach?
   a. a great championship team
   b. a newly formed team
   c. a losing team
   d. a team with a weak offense

Passage 23

Frankenstein is a well-known horror tale about a monster. Frankenstein films and books have scared and thrilled millions, young and old.

The original story was written over 160 years ago by a 19-year old girl, Mary Godwin. Mary later married the poet Shelley. Mary began her story one dark, stormy summer night. She was living with friends in a house on a lake in Switzerland. They were sitting by the fire telling ghost stories. The poet Byron said that they should write ghost stories of their own.

Mary's story came to her that night in a dream. When it was finished months later, she named it *Frankenstein*. The book was published two years after she had started it. She did not put her name on it. Readers did not know that it had been written by a woman.

In her story a scientist named Frankenstein has discovered the secret of life. He decides to create a man. Instead he creates a horrible monster. He is unable to control this monster and is murdered by him.

The first Frankenstein movie was a silent film. It was produced in 1910 by Thomas Alva Edison, the inventor. In 1931 a sound film was produced. It was very popular and made millions of dollars for the producers. Many other Frankenstein films followed. They also drew large audiences and were very profitable. In these films the story is different from the original one written by Mary Godwin Shelley.

When Frankenstein films were shown on TV they, too, became very popular.

Passage 23

1. To complete her book it took Mary Godwin Shelley
    a. one night.
    b. one month.
    c. less than two years.
    d. more than two years.

2. In her book Frankenstein is the name of
    a. a famous scientist.
    b. the monster.
    c. a friend of the author.
    d. the author.

3. We can conclude that Frankenstein films became popular because people like stories that are
    a. funny.
    b. sad.
    c. scary.
    d. romantic.

4. It has been said that this book was the beginning of books that today are called
    a. mysteries.
    b. science fiction.
    c. detective stories.
    d. adventure stories.

Passage 24

The first people to cross the Atlantic by balloon were Ben Abruzzo, Max Anderson, and Larry Newman. The flight from Presque Isle, Maine to Misery, France in August, 1978 took five days and 17 hours.

The balloonists had spent thousands of hours practicing for the flight. All three men were expert pilots. This was Ben Abruzzo's and Max Anderson's second attempt to cross the Atlantic by balloon. Larry Newman, though, was new to ballooning.

They called their craft *Double Eagle II*. They named it after Charles Lindbergh, whose nickname was the Lone Eagle. Lindbergh was the first person to cross the Atlantic on a solo airflight.

The *Double Eagle* was 11 stories high. It was made up of two parts—a balloon and a gondola. The red and yellow gondola had a twin-hulled boat that could float if necessary.

For breakfast during the trip the men had doughnuts, raisins, and coffee or cocoa. Later in the day they ate high protein sardines and hot dogs. They also took lots of vitamins.

It was not an easy flight. The temperature in the gondola went down to zero. The men used a portable heater to prevent frostbite.

Once they neared the coast of France, though, they forgot about their discomfort. Small planes and helicopters met them and formed an honor guard to escort them to France. A large crowd welcomed them there.

The flight cost these three men $125,000. Why had they done it? Ben Abruzzo said, "Unless frontiers are challenged—we don't move forward as a society."

Passage 24

1. The balloonists made this flight
   a. to show that balloons were easy to fly.
   b. to win a large prize.
   c. because no one had ever done it before.
   d. to make their families proud of them.

2. What showed that these men were prepared to land on water? They had their
   a. oxygen masks.
   b. balloon.
   c. gondola.
   d. supply of food.

3. We can conclude that ballooning is
   a. an expensive sport.
   b. a safe sport.
   c. a very popular sport.
   d. a sport for young people only.

4. This passage tells us that the men took special
   a. clothing and radios.
   b. clothing and food.
   c. food and heating equipment.
   d. books and maps.

Passage 25

Charlie Brown and the gang had their 25th birthday in October, 1975. The *Peanuts* comic strips seem to get more popular every year. They are read by millions of readers each day in over 1,800 newspapers all over the world. They are translated into more than ten languages.

Charlie Brown and the gang are also the stars of hundreds of books. They are seen on TV and in movies. There are all kinds of Charlie Brown products, such as toys, clothing, cards, and blankets.

Peanuts has no adults. Children and animals are the main characters. Yet grownups are among its most enthusiastic admirers. The characters are very real. Young and old want to hear all about Charlie Brown, Lucy, Linus, and Snoopy.

The author of this popular cartoon is Charles Schultz. He is known by his nickname, Sparky. He was born in 1922 in Minnesota, where he grew up. His father liked comic strips and bought four Sunday newspapers with comic strips. Sparky loved to draw. He liked the Disney characters and kept on drawing them.

During his last year in high school he tried to sell his cartoon strips, but he had no success. His great success came much later, in 1950. He sold his comic strip, *Li'l Folks*. The syndicate that bought it called it *Peanuts*.

Schultz is very fond of Charlie Brown and his other cartoon characters. He is careful about the Charlie Brown items that he endorses. They must meet his high standards.

Schultz does all the drawing himself. He keeps ten weeks ahead on the Sunday strip, six weeks ahead on the daily. About drawing cartoons he says, "It's my life."

Passage 25

1. Choose the best answer.
   Charlie Brown cartoons are enjoyed by
   a. children.
   b. teenagers.
   c. people of all ages.
   d. grownups.

2. Schultz became a successful cartoonist
   a. immediately.
   b. when he was almost 30 years old.
   c. because he had many talented assistants.
   d. during his high school years.

3. We can conclude that Schultz
   a. cares only about making money.
   b. loves children and animals.
   c. prefers grownups.
   d. dislikes people.

4. Choose the best answer.
   People buy Charlie Brown items because they
   a. like well-made items.
   b. love the characters.
   c. want inexpensive items.
   d. want to buy what's popular.

Passage 26

Langston Hughes, who died in 1967, was a black American writer. During his lifetime people all over the world, old and young, read and enjoyed what he wrote. He has remained popular because his writings show the speech, the feelings, and the thoughts of the black people of his time.

His first book of poems, *The Weary Blues*, was published when he was 24 years old. These poems and the poems he wrote later were different from those written by other black poets. He wrote about life as it really was. He used new forms of verse. Some of his poems had the rhythm of blues songs, jazz, or spirituals.

Besides poetry, Hughes wrote short stories, history, novels, plays, and autobiography. He wrote for newspapers and magazines, for radio and TV. More than 40 volumes of his work were published.

Hughes wrote so well because he told about the people he knew best. He gave lifelike pictures of them. He wrote about life in the slums, poor parts of the cities where many black people lived. He had lived in those slums. He knew what it was like to be poor. He had been a laundry worker, a farm helper, a dishwasher, and a waiter. He had worked on ships, too.

Langston Hughes wanted it to be possible for all people to enjoy freedom. Through his writing he hoped he could help improve the lives and working conditions of his people.

Although he had many hardships in his life, he never lost his sense of humor. His readers enjoy the humor that is found in much of his work.

Passage 26

1. The best title for this passage is
   a. A Famous Poet.
   b. A Famous Black Poet.
   c. A Famous Black Author.
   d. A Famous Black American Author.

2. Most of Hughes' writing was about
   a. important black people.
   b. poor black people.
   c. poor white people.
   d. black people who lived in the country.

3. From this passage we can conclude that Hughes was a
   a. person who disliked work.
   b. man who never laughed.
   c. cold, unfeeling man.
   d. warm, understanding man.

4. From this passage we can conclude that Hughes
   a. liked music.
   b. liked art.
   c. did not like dancing.
   d. did not like movies and plays.

Passage 27

Belva Lockwood was a champion of women's rights and the world peace movement.

She was born in New York State in 1830. When she was 19 she married. Four years later her husband died. She taught school to support herself and her daughter. Later, she graduated from college. At that time this was unusual. She became head of a school district in New York.

Belva Lockwood met Susan B. Anthony, a leader of the women's rights movement. This meeting increased her own interest in this movement. In 1866 she moved to Washington, D.C. She opened her own school. Two years later she remarried. She wanted to study law. Her husband encouraged her. At first no school would take her because she was a woman. Then a new law school admitted her.

After she graduated she opened a law practice. Because she was a woman, Belva Lockwood was not allowed to plead a case before a federal court. She lobbied against this in Congress. In 1879 a law was passed which gave women lawyers the right to practice in all courts.

She helped pass other state and federal laws which increased women's rights. In 1884 a woman's group nominated Belva Lockwood for president of the United States. By the late 1880s she was sure that women would win their fight for equal rights. She devoted her time to supporting the world peace movement.

Throughout the years she had her own law practice. When she was 75 she represented the Eastern Cherokee Indians in a suit against the United States government. The court granted the Indians five million dollars.

Belva Lockwood died at the age of 86.

Passage 27

1. Choose the best title.
   a. Belva Lockwood, a Leader of Women's Rights
   b. Belva Lockwood, First Woman Lawyer
   c. The Women's Rights Movement
   d. The First Female Candidate for President.

2. Belva Lockwood did not work for
   a. the world peace movement.
   b. the women's rights movement.
   c. the nuclear disarmament movement.
   d. the American Indians' movement.

3. Choose the best answer.
   We can conclude that Belva Lockwood was
   a. very shy.
   b. impatient.
   c. an excellent speaker.
   d. not easily defeated.

4. Which group of people would be most influenced by Belva Lockwood's career?
   a. male lawyers
   b. female lawyers
   c. teachers
   d. members of Congress

Passage 28

Citizen's Band, or C.B. radios have become very popular in recent years. There are about 25 million of these radios in this country. Many homes have them. At least half of the trucks in the United States are equipped with them. They are used in about one of every eight cars.

The C.B. radio is easy to set up and use. You need a radio, an aerial, an antenna mast for the home station, and a power source. The power source is the home electrical system or car. The radio is connected to a power set and turned on. You move the tuner to the channel you want. Then you press the send button and speak into the microphone.

C.B. fans have developed their own language. A radio is called a *raddidio*. A state trooper is a *Smokey Bear*. A tunnel is a *hole-in-the-wall*. C.B. fans have a dictionary that lists C.B. words and meanings.

C.B. radios have many good uses. If a family has one in their car and at home they can keep in touch with one another. C.B. radios can help a driver who is in trouble. If the car breaks down, the person can get help by using the radio.

C.B.'s can aid in highway safety. Drivers warn one another of dangerous spots on a road. Truck drivers who travel long distances talk on the radio to other drivers. This helps them stay awake and avoid accidents.

Unfortunately, drivers can also use their C.B. radios to warn one another of an approaching police car or a police checkpoint.

Passage 28

1. Choose the best answer.
   C.B. radios are popular because they
   a. have had so much publicity.
   b. can be used in many ways.
   c. are better than telephones.
   d. have their own language.

2. The C.B. radio is most popular with
   a. car owners.
   b. truck drivers.
   c. motorcyle owners.
   d. trailer owners.

3. The C.B. radio would be a good present for a
   a. small child.
   b. person who rarely drives.
   c. lonely, bed-ridden person.
   d. person who dislikes other people.

4. Choose the best answer.
   We can conclude that in the future
   a. owners of C.B. radios may need licenses.
   b. C.B. radios may become less popular.
   c. the government may forbid the use of all C.B. radios.
   d. the police may want all cars to have C.B. radios.

Passage 29

Dolphins have excellent hearing. Like people, they have five senses. Scientists have found that hearing is the most important of the dolphin's five senses. Dolphins depend on their hearing as people depend on their sight.

How do they hear? They make a set of quick clicks. These clicks travel through the water. When the clicks reach a solid object, they bounce off it and return to the dolphin. Dolphins can hear these echoes clearly and can tell that solid objects are nearby. They can locate the objects and tell their size and shape. A blindfolded dolphin was able to find half a vitamin pill on the bottom of its tank.

Dr. Winthrop Kellogg did a famous study of dolphins. For six years he experimented in an outdoor pool with two dolphins, Albert and Betty. He made important discoveries.

He found that dolphins send off clicking noises every 15 to 20 seconds. Through these clicks dolphins hear and keep careful watch on their pool. He found that their hearing is so sharp that they could hear when half a teaspoonful of water was dropped into the pool.

They could tell what was put into the water. If a fish was dropped the dolphins swam toward it. The dolphins could also tell one fish from another by size. For example, Albert did not like a mullet, a 12-inch fish. He did like a spot, a 6-inch fish. When a spot and mullet were dropped into the water at the same time he could tell them apart.

As scientists learn more about dolphins and sound waves, they hope to be able to apply this knowledge to help people.

Passage 29

1. Choose the best answer.
   Dolphins' hearing depends on
   a. their ears.
   b. clicks.
   c. echoes.
   d. clicks and echoes.

2. According to this passage much has been learned about dolphins from a
   a. study made in an aquarium.
   b. book written by a scientist.
   c. study made in an outdoor pool.
   d. film on dolphins.

3. We can conclude that dolphins can tell the difference between a
   a. fish with gray skin and a fish with white skin.
   b. fish with scales and a fish without scales.
   c. male and a female turtle.
   d. small fish and a large fish.

4. We can conclude that the scientists who discovered how dolphins hear must have
   a. been rich.
   b. had patience.
   c. had luck.
   d. liked to swim.

Passage 30

Harry Houdini was a master of magic and escape tricks. Houdini's real name was Ehrich Weiss. Born in Hungary in 1874, he came to this country as a baby. In America people called him Harry.

When he was a teenager Harry worked as an assistant tie cutter. In his free time he learned magic tricks. He read a book by Robert Houdin, a great magician. This book had a great effect on him. Harry admired Houdin so much that he changed his name to Houdini. Then, at 17, he quit his job and became a full-time magician.

He performed in circuses and small shows. He wasn't very successful until he met Martin Beck, a famous producer. Beck told Houdini to concentrate on doing escape tricks. Soon Houdini was a huge success.

Houdini's escape tricks thrilled the audiences. His most famous trick was the Water-Torture Cell. He was put upside down in a small box in a tank of water. His ankles were put in ankle holes. Then the tank was locked and steel bands put around it. If he did not escape in two minutes he would drown.

To advertise his act Houdini staged escapes from many public places. For example, in 1906 he went to a Boston jail. He was handcuffed and his legs were put in irons. He was then locked up in a cell. Minutes later he escaped.

Houdini was also a wonderful magician. In his best-known act he swallowed two packages of needles and some thread. After taking a swallow of water he opened his mouth. Out came evenly threaded needles.

No wonder he was called the Great Houdini!

Passage 30

1. Who helped Houdini to become a successful magician?
   a. Martin Beck
   b. Robert Houdin
   c. Ehrich Weiss
   d. his father

2. Houdini realized that to be a success he needed
   a. good luck.
   b. good advertising.
   c. expensive equipment.
   d. help from other magicians.

3. Whom would Houdini's skills help most?
   a. pilots
   b. bus drivers
   c. policemen
   d. teachers

4. Choose the best answer.
   We can conclude that Houdini's acts were popular because
   a. they were very exciting.
   b. they showed some skill.
   c. circus acts were admired at the time.
   d. he wore unusual costumes.

Passage 31

England held a great celebration in June, 1977. It was called the Silver Jubilee. The British marked their queen's 25th year on the throne.

Queen Elizabeth opened the week-long festival. She lit a 30-foot bonfire near Windsor Castle. Then more than 100 bonfires were lit throughout Great Britain.

In London there was a church service. The Queen and her husband, Prince Philip, led the parade from Buckingham Palace to St. Paul's Cathedral. They rode in a gold state coach driven by eight gray horses. The great coach was accompanied by coachmen, knights, and troops. They wore brilliantly-colored uniforms. More than a million people watched the long parade.

At the Cathedral the royal family was greeted by music played on eight silver trumpets. Special hymns and sermons marked the service. The Queen and Prince Philip sat on gilt and red velvet armchairs.

The costumes of those at St. Paul's varied. The Archbishop of Canterbury wore his tall red-and-gold cap. The Lord Chamberlain and the Speaker of the House of Commons wore gold-and-black gowns and long gray wigs. City officials wore robes richly trimmed with sable. The gentlemen-at-arms had brass helmets with white plumes.

In all parts of the kingdom huge crowds rejoiced while church bells rang. In her speeches the Queen pledged to continue to serve her people. This jubilee was more than a huge national party. It showed the great respect and affection which most people feel for their queen.

Passage 31

1. The British celebrated their queen's 25th anniversary on the throne because they
   a. respect and love the queen.
   b. love parades.
   c. wanted a long holiday.
   d. wanted to see the gold coach.

2. Choose the best answer.
   Celebrations were held
   a. in London.
   b. at Windsor Castle.
   c. at Buckingham Palace.
   d. throughout the British Isles.

3. We can conclude that
   a. the British like their form of government.
   b. the British would like a government like ours.
   c. the Church has no place in British life.
   d. celebrations in England are very simple.

4. We can conclude that the Queen
   a. takes her duties seriously.
   b. cares only about having a good time.
   c. travels without Prince Philip.
   d. is against religion.

Passage 32

In 1976 an 86-pound, 14-year old Rumanian gymnast was the star of the Olympic Games. The Games were held in Montreal. People watching Nadia Comaneci perform were amazed at her skill and grace. She was fearless and tireless.

Nadia was declared the world's best all-around gymnast. She had seven perfect scores. She won three gold medals and a bronze medal.

In Rumania sports are an important part of the schools' programs. The government wants to train children to enter the Olympic Games. They are always looking for young children who like sports and are good at them. These children have special programs.

When she was six years old Nadia was one of those chosen. She had three to four hours of hard practice daily after school.

When she was 11 years old she started winning championships. Three years later she was the champion of Europe.

Nadia has a strict diet. She eats fruit, milk, cheese, and other protein foods. She does not eat bread or foods with sugar. It is said that at banquets during a United States tour she ate only salads.

After her fantastic record in the 1976 Olympic Games the small young star returned home. There the president of her country gave her a special gold medal. This was the highest honor. She also received letters and presents from people from all over the world.

She was a world champion. Her school program, though, remained the same. She went back to a full high school course. She also had to continue her special routine of gymnastics.

Passage 32

1. Choose the best answer.
   The audience at the Olympic Games was most impressed by Nadia's
   a. good looks.
   b. youth.
   c. grace.
   d. perfect scores.

2. Choose the best answer.
   The young Rumanians who compete in athletic tournaments are so well prepared because
   a. their schools give strict sports training.
   b. they come from a better climate.
   c. they eat better food.
   d. they are born with talent in sports.

3. We can conclude that Nadia
   a. has a lot of self-control.
   b. is conceited.
   c. cares most about making money.
   d. is unselfish.

4. We can conclude that Nadia's coaches believed in the saying
   a. Don't cry over spilt milk.
   b. Practice makes perfect.
   c. Better late than never.
   d. Many hands make light work.

Passage 33

Freshwater eels are snakelike fish. They have a long, thin shape, slimy skin, and tiny scales. They are from one to five feet long. They are brown or green in color.

For centuries scientists had tried to find out about them. No one had ever seen a freshwater fish lay an egg. Nobody knew where they came from or how the babies were born. The mystery surrounding these fish was solved in 1932.

A Danish scientist had been looking for 18 years for the eggs of freshwater eels. He finally found the eels' spawning place, the place where they shed their eggs. He found newly born tiny larvae. Larvae are hatched eggs.

He found them in the Sargasso Sea in the western Atlantic Ocean near Bermuda. He discovered that, although these eels live in fresh water, they mate and reproduce in salt water. To get to the sea the eels travel long distances. They go from lakes or rivers in the eastern and central regions of the United States. Some travel over 1,000 miles.

The female produces millions of eggs. They are the size of pin heads. The adult eels die after spawning. Those larvae that rise from the depths of the sea are only about one quarter of an inch long. They are flat, thin, and as clear as glass.

When the larvae are about two and a half inches long, their bodies change. Because they are still as transparent as glass, they are called glass eels. These slowly drift toward the lakes and rivers of the United States. When the eels that survive the long trip arrive about a year later, they are fully grown adult eels.

Passage 33

1. Scientists started to study freshwater eels
   a. hundreds of years ago.
   b. in the 1800s.
   c. in the 1930s.
   d. in the 1970s.

2. As they develop, the size of freshwater eels changes
   a. very little.
   b. somewhat.
   c. a great deal.
   d. not at all.

3. It took many years to find out about freshwater eels because scientists did not look in
   a. lakes.
   b. rivers.
   c. ponds.
   d. the sea.

4. Scientists found it hardest to believe that
   a. eels produce so many eggs.
   b. the eggs of eels are so tiny.
   c. eels can get to the sea.
   d. eels look like snakes.

Passage 34

Baseball fans remember Hank Aaron as one of the greatest sluggers of all time. In 1974, when he hit his 715th home run, he became baseball's home run record holder.

Hank was born in Mobile, Alabama, in 1934. He always loved baseball. His father, who had been a semi-professional ballplayer, taught Hank the game.

When Hank Aaron was 18 he joined the Indianapolis Clowns, of the Negro National League. While he played for them his hitting improved. He changed his grip so that he could hit better and he developed his almost perfect timing.

In 1952 he joined a farm club of the Milwaukee Braves. He also switched from shortstop to outfield. In 1954, when their regular outfielder was hurt, Hank Aaron became a Braves outfielder.

He did well from the start. By 1959 he was leading the league in hitting. In 1972 he earned $200,000 a year. He was the highest paid player in baseball.

In addition to playing ball he spent a lot of time helping other people. He taught baseball and basketball to kids. He was also active in trying to find a cure for sickle cell anemia.

Although Hank Aaron is remembered mainly for his home run record, he also broke many other records. He collected more total bases, more extra base hits, and more sacrifice flies than any other player. He also holds the record for more bases on balls and more runs batted in.

When he was asked to explain his great batting skill, Hank Aaron said, "I just leave the dugout swinging. The secret of hitting is to keep swinging."

Passage 34

1. Choose the best title.
   a. The Life of a Star
   b. Home Run Kings
   c. Hank Aaron, A Baseball Great
   d. A Baseball Player

2. Hank Aaron's hitting style
   a. never changed.
   b. changed when he was a young player.
   c. was perfect from the start.
   d. took many years to develop.

3. We can conclude that Hank Aaron is
   a. lazy.
   b. selfish.
   c. generous.
   d. handsome.

4. We can conclude that Hank Aaron's most successful year was
   a. 1934.
   b. 1952.
   c. 1959.
   d. 1974.

Passage 35

The Bermuda Triangle is an area of the western Atlantic Ocean where many ships and planes have disappeared. At first the Triangle was drawn with imaginary lines. These lines went from Miami to Bermuda, from Bermuda to Puerto Rico, and from Puerto Rico to Miami. Because many sea and air disappearances took place beyond this Triangle the area was enlarged.

Christopher Columbus was the first person to write about this area. He wrote that the currents were strange. They seemed to move his ships against the wind.

The mystery has continued. Over the years people have noticed the high number of strange ship losses in the Triangle. Large ships with hundreds of people on board have vanished. Small ships have been lost, too.

In the early days of air travel many small planes vanished. Even when air travel became more advanced there were still many plane losses. At first these ship and plane losses were thought of as separate events.

During the 1940s, though, people began to think that there might be a special problem with this part of the Atlantic. They noted that the ships and planes never gave distress calls. In fact, they never gave any signs of trouble. For the most part no traces of the lost crafts were found.

Many people blame the ocean itself. It can suddenly become very dangerous. Waterspouts, swift currents, and eddies appear quickly. There are also strange weather conditions in this area. Sudden winds, violent storms, and hurricanes appear.

Some people wonder if perhaps a mysterious force affects the Triangle.

Passage 35

1. Choose the best answer.
   The Bermuda Triangle was first written about
   a. over 100 years ago.
   b. over 200 years ago.
   c. over 300 years ago.
   d. over 400 years ago.

2. Choose the sentence that best explains the Bermuda Triangle accidents.
   a. Everyone thinks that the ocean causes them.
   b. Everyone thinks that poor weather causes them.
   c. Everyone thinks unknown forces cause them.
   d. There is no proven reason for them.

3. We can conclude that when people fly over the Triangle
   a. everyone is afraid.
   b. no one worries.
   c. some people are afraid.
   d. everyone takes out flight insurance.

4. The Triangle would not affect the tourist business in
   a. Bermuda.
   b. Miami.
   c. New York.
   d. Puerto Rico.

Passage 36

Milton Hershey made chocolate a well-known food in this country. He was born in 1857. At 15 he worked for a candymaker in Lancaster, Pennsylvania. Hershey liked the candy business. He loved mixing all the ingredients together and then watching and testing the candy.

At 19 Hershey went to Philadelphia to start his own business, but he couldn't make enough money to pay his expenses. He was forced to close his shop.

Hershey then moved to Denver. He worked for a candymaker who taught him a new way to make caramels. He used fresh milk. It made them taste better. It made them chewier and longer lasting, too.

In 1883 Hershey started a candy business in New York. People liked his milk caramels, but again he had money problems. His business failed. He had just enough money to get home to Lancaster. There he borrowed some money. He made caramels and sold them from a basket on the street.

One day an English candy importer ate one of Hershey's candies. He offered to sell them in England. Soon Hershey's business was a great success.

In 1893 he attended a large fair in Chicago. He saw chocolate-making equipment. He decided to make chocolates, too.

In 1900 Hershey sold his caramel business. He decided to concentrate on making chocolates. Milk chocolate had never been made in this country. He decided to make one chocolate item and to produce it in great quantities. He wanted it to be so cheap that everyone could buy it. His famous Hershey Chocolate Bar was an immediate success!

Passage 36

1. Hershey made his first fortune from
   a. chocolate kisses.
   b. chocolate bars.
   c. taffy.
   d. caramels.

2. Hershey became a success because
   a. he was open to new ideas.
   b. he started out with a few shops.
   c. he had good luck.
   d. he had a lot of money.

3. We can conclude that the Hershey Chocolate Bar was popular because it
   a. was full of vitamins.
   b. came in many sizes.
   c. tasted good and was cheap.
   d. tasted better than dark chocolate.

4. We can conclude that Hershey believed in the saying
   a. If at first you don't succeed, try, try again.
   b. Don't make a mountain out of a molehill.
   c. People in glass houses shouldn't throw stones.
   d. A rolling stone gathers no moss.

Passage 37

Muhammad Ali was the first person to win the heavyweight boxing title three times.

He was born in Kentucky in 1942.

The story of how Ali started in boxing is an interesting one. When he was 12 his bike was stolen. Ali told a policeman that he wanted to beat up the thief. The policeman advised him to learn to box first. The policeman taught boxing and invited Ali to join his class. Six weeks later Ali was in his first amateur fight. From then on his goal was to become the world champion.

By the time he finished high school Ali had fought in over 100 fights. He lost only six of them. He won the National Golden Gloves Championship twice.

In 1960, when he was only 18, he won the Olympic gold medal in boxing. After the Olympics Ali turned pro. He was the fastest heavyweight boxer anyone had ever seen.

Muhammad Ali began to write rhymes praising himself. He boasted, "They all must fall in the round I call." When he was 22 he became the world's heavyweight champion.

During the Vietnam war he was drafted into the Army. He did not believe in the war. He refused to join the Army, was stripped of his title, and was not allowed to fight for four years. A jury found him guilty of evading the draft. Later, however, the Supreme Court said that he had the right to refuse to fight.

In 1971 he challenged the world's heavyweight champion. After a long, tough fight Ali was defeated. Four years later, though, he became heavyweight champion again. In 1978 he lost his title, but a few months later he became champion for the third time.

Passage 37

1. As a fighter Muhammad Ali was known for his
   a. grace.
   b. strength.
   c. speed.
   d. temper.

2. Ali first started to box when he was in
   a. junior high school.
   b. high school.
   c. college.
   d. the army.

3. Ali's refusal to join the Army showed that he was
   a. willing to stand up for what he believed in.
   b. a coward.
   c. against all wars.
   d. not a patriot.

4. The story of the stolen bike and the policeman is an example of
   a. good coming out of evil.
   b. good coming out of good.
   c. evil coming out of good.
   d. evil coming out of evil.

Passage 38

In 1915 Great Britain was at war with Germany. Great Britain controlled the seas. Germany wanted to cut off the shipments of food and supplies that were going to Great Britain. These came on ships from all parts of the British empire. Germany used submarines to attack them. Germany told the submarine captains to sink all ships at sight.

Without warning a German submarine torpedoed the British liner *Lusitania* on May 7, 1915. There was an explosion and fire. The ship went down off the Irish coast. It sank in half an hour. 1,198 passengers and crew were killed. Among those who lost their lives were 128 Americans.

Under international law the passengers and crew of a passenger ship had to be rescued. Small submarines, though, could not do this. The sinking and loss of lives shocked the world. Americans were very angry.

Before the sinking of this great ship President Wilson had warned Germany. He had said that the United States would hold it responsible for the loss of any American ships or lives. After the sinking he threatened to break off relations with Germany. The two countries were near war. Germany did not want us to come into the war. It said it would warn us before sinking ships that were not warships. President Wilson tried to stay out of the war.

However on April 6, 1917, the United States entered the war. President Wilson had asked Congress to declare war. One of his reasons was that Germany was waging submarine warfare against all ships. It had sunk four American ships. This declaration of war came 17 months after the sinking of the *Lusitania.*

Passage 38

1. Which country had the greatest sea power in 1915?
   a. Germany
   b. Great Britain
   c. France
   d. the United States

2. The world was angry when the *Lusitania* was sunk because of the loss of
   a. an expensive ship.
   b. so many of the crew.
   c. so many of the British navy.
   d. so many of the passengers and crew.

3. We can conclude that President Wilson was
   a. a man who wanted war.
   b. a peace-loving man.
   c. a cowardly man.
   d. a man with a quick temper.

4. We can conclude that a major reason for the United States' entering the war in 1917 was:
   a. Great Britain was losing and needed our help.
   b. A war would give jobs to many people.
   c. Germany was attacking American ships.
   d. The people in the United States wanted war.

Passage 39

Chris Evert is one of the world's best tennis players. She has won four straight United States Open Titles. For four years in a row she has been named the best women's player. She has been the victor in 113 straight tennis matches on clay courts.

Chris Evert comes from a family of tennis players. When Chris was five her father taught her to hit tennis balls against a cement wall. Then he gave her lessons.

From the start Chris was a winner. When she was only eight she won her first big award. At 16 she was the youngest player to reach the semifinals of the national championships at Forest Hills.

Chris decided to become a professional player. When she was 18 she played her first professional match. This was the S & H Green Stamps Women's Tennis Classics. It was held in Ft. Lauderdale, her hometown. She won, and her prize was $10,000.

A year later Chris Evert won her first Wimbledon Singles Championship. She was ranked the world's best woman tennis player. The next year she earned a record sum of $367,227 in prize money and was voted female athlete of the year.

Great skill and concentration make Chris Evert a champion. She has a great baseline game, a steady ground stroke, and a strong serve. However, her clear thinking and concentration are her strongest features.

Margaret Court, another great tennis player, says of Chris: "She concentrates to the last point. It makes her a champion. Even when she is losing, she concentrates and doesn't give up."

Passage 39

1. The best title for this story is
   a. A Wimbledon Champion
   b. A Pro Player
   c. A Money Winner
   d. Chris Evert

2. The greatest influence on Chris' early tennis career was
   a. her school.
   b. her coach.
   c. her father.
   d. her family.

3. Chris first became a winner when she was in
   a. elementary school.
   b. junior high school.
   c. high school.
   d. college.

4. We can conclude that tennis
   a. is easy to learn.
   b. is played only in the summer.
   c. can be a profitable sport.
   d. is played only in the United States.

Passage 40

The marathon, or long-distance race, can be traced back to ancient Greece. In 490 B.C. a Greek soldier ran from Marathon to Athens, a distance of over 22 miles. He brought news of his country's defeat of the Persians.

When the first modern Olympic Games were held in Greece in 1896 the founders remembered this ancient soldier. There was a race from Marathon to Athens. This was the first modern marathon.

Through the years Olympic marathons varied in length. In 1908, though, it was decided that runners would have to run 26 miles, 385 yards.

In that year the Olympics were held in Great Britain. The extra 385 yards were added to the race so that the starting line would be at the walls of Windsor Castle, the home of the royal family. Thus, the royal family had a good view of the race. Later, this became the official Olympic distance.

Boston held the first American marathon in 1897. Most of the runners were local men. Machinists, milkmen, and farmers ran almost 25 miles over dirt roads. Because of poor conditions and training their speed was much slower than that of today's runners. Since that first race the Boston Marathon has been a yearly event.

Through the years marathons have been started in other places. The distance varies with each race. Only the Olympics has a set marathon distance.

In the 1970s marathon racing started to be popular in this country. There was a growing interest in physical fitness. In 1970 127 people ran in the New York Marathon, in 1978 there were 11,400 runners!

Passage 40

1. Choose the best title.
   a. Marathon Running in the United States
   b. Olympic Marathon Races
   c. Marathons Become Popular
   d. The History of Marathon Races

2. The Olympic Marathon is 26 miles, 385 yards because that was the distance
   a. from Marathon to Athens.
   b. of the Boston Marathon.
   c. needed to please British royalty.
   d. the Olympic Committee wanted.

3. We can conclude that a company making running shoes earned the most money
   a. in the 1890s.
   b. in the 1920s.
   c. in the 1950s.
   d. in the 1970s.

4. Who was probably the fastest runner?
   a. the ancient Greek soldier
   b. the winner of the 1896 Olympic Marathon
   c. the winner of the 1897 Boston Marathon
   d. the winner of the 1978 New York Marathon

Passage 41

Charlie Chaplin was one of the greatest film stars of all times. He was born in a London slum in 1888. His father was an actor and his mother was a singer.

Even as a child, Charlie wanted to act. At five he replaced his mother on stage when her voice failed. Later he danced in the streets for pennies. As a teenager he had many acting jobs.

By 1913, when Chaplin was 24, he was doing well as a comedian with an English variety show. The show toured the United States. A movie producer saw the show. He offered Chaplin a job in movie comedies.

In 1914 Chaplin invented a film character called The Little Tramp. The Little Tramp starred in Chaplin's films for about 25 years. People recognized him because he always wore pants and shoes that were too large for him. He wore a derby and carried a cane. The Little Tramp had many problems, but always hoped for a better future. Fans loved him.

Chaplin soon was earning $670,000 a year. He was probably the world's highest paid performer. In 1917 he helped form United Artists Studios. From then on, he had complete control of his pictures. He wrote, produced, and acted in them.

Chaplin believed that acting and photography should be simple. He told actors not to act, but just to be natural. He felt that one camera shot could tell a whole story. Because of Chaplin, simplicity became the style in acting and in camera work.

Many people say Chaplin was "the greatest film artist in motion picture history."

Passage 41

1. Chaplin earned worldwide fame when he was
   a. a small child.
   b. a teenager.
   c. a young man.
   d. a middle-aged man.

2. Chaplin thought that a film actor should
   a. be simple.
   b. be very dramatic.
   c. move around a lot.
   d. show no emotion.

3. We can conclude that in the future
   a. audiences will continue to enjoy Chaplin films.
   b. audiences will be bored with Chaplin's films.
   c. audiences will think that Chaplin's films are too old-fashioned.
   d. very few movie houses will show Chaplin films.

4. Choose the best answer.
   We remember Charlie Chaplin because he was
   a. a famous street dancer.
   b. a good stage comedian.
   c. a genius in the making of movies.
   d. the inventor of sound movies.

Passage 42

Americans like fast foods and buy lots of them. When driving, people may stop to eat at fast food shops. People like to eat fast foods at home, too. Some fast foods are cooked and ready to take out. Thousands of take-out food stores are located throughout the country. They are on highways, in big cities, and in small towns.

Among the best-known fast foods are hot dogs, hamburgers, French fries, fried chicken, fish and chips, pizza, chili, and tacos. Nutritionists who study food and health are concerned about the regular eating of this kind of food. Much of it is fried. Much of it contains too much fat and starch and too much salt.

Children know about fast food chains from radio and TV advertising. These ads affect the kinds of foods kids want to eat. Some may want only hamburgers with ketchup. Others may ask for hot dogs on a roll. If they want some chicken, they may settle only for fried chicken.

Fast food meals cost less than other restaurant meals. Usually there is no tipping. Adults may prefer them because they require no marketing, no cooking, and very little cleanup.

When people — both adults and children — eat mainly fast foods, they probably don't eat enough whole grains, dairy products, fresh fruits, and vegetables. Their diet is not varied enough to provide all the vitamins and minerals which the body needs. Fortunately, though, some people are growing more aware of the effect of the food they eat on their health. They are paying more attention to diet.

Passage 42

1. The best title for this passage is
   a. The Popularity of Fast Foods.
   b. The Popularity of Hamburgers.
   c. Fresh Fruits and Vegetables.
   d. Fast Food Stores in Cities.

2. Parents like fast food stores because
   a. they enjoy taking their children to restaurants.
   b. their children get well-balanced meals.
   c. their children like them.
   d. tipping is never allowed.

3. From this passage the reader can conclude that
   a. radio and TV advertising is not always in the best interests of children.
   b. radio and TV advertising has very little effect on children
   c. radio and TV advertising is not expensive
   d. there are few radio and TV ads for fast foods.

4. From this passage the reader can conclude that
   a. good cooks recommend fast food stores.
   b. fast foods contain all the vitamins necessary for good health.
   c. people should be more concerned about the food they eat.
   d. parents who take their children to fast food stores are good parents.

Passage 43

Marian Anderson, the famous singer, was born in Philadelphia in 1902. Even as a baby she could carry a tune. When she was only six, Marian joined her church choir. In her teens she was earning money singing.

Marian needed voice training lessons. Her church raised money to send her to a music school. Because she was black she was not allowed to register. Instead she took lessons from a black singer. Later she trained with a well-known voice coach.

Marian thought of becoming an opera singer, but her coach discouraged her. In those days black people were not welcome in opera companies. In 1925 she entered a singing contest. Of the 300 singers who competed she placed first.

She went to Europe to study. She stayed there several years. In 1931 when she went on her first European singing tour, she was a great hit! Then she realized that she could be a success as a concert singer even though she was black.

In 1935 Marian Anderson returned home. Her concerts got rave reviews. She was a great star. In 1939, though, she was not allowed to sing at a famous hall in Washington, D.C. because she was black. The government then asked her to sing at the Lincoln Memorial. 75,000 people came to hear her. In 1955 she fulfilled an early dream. She became the first black person to sing with the Metropolitan Opera.

Marian Anderson retired in 1965. People who heard her, though, never forgot her voice. It thrilled millions of people. A great conductor said that it was a voice heard "once in a 100 years."

Passage 43

1. During her early career Marian Anderson's greatest problem was
   a. her color.
   b. her sex.
   c. her poor training.
   d. her lack of money.

2. Choose the best answer.
   Marian Anderson's European tour was important because she
   a. made a lot of money.
   b. learned about different countries.
   c. found out that her color was not a handicap.
   d. learned more about music.

3. We can conclude that Marian Anderson was
   a. shy.
   b. ambitious.
   c. weak.
   d. selfish.

4. Marian Anderson became a famous singer because she
   a. had great natural talent.
   b. had excellent teachers.
   c. went to Europe.
   d. had good luck.

Progress Graph

	1	2	3	4	5	6	7	8	9	10	11	12	13	14	15	16	17	18
4 CORRECT = 100%																		
3 CORRECT = 75%																		
2 CORRECT = 50%																		
1 CORRECT = 25%																		

19	20	21	22	23	24	25	26	27	28	29	30	31	32	33	34	35	36	37	38	39	40	41	42	43

Answer Sheet

PASSAGE	QUESTION 1	QUESTION 2	QUESTION 3	QUESTION 4
1	b	b	d	c
2	b	b	d	a
3	c	d	d	b
4	d	a	d	c
5	b	a	c	d
6	c	a	a	c
7	b	a	a	b
8	c	a	b	b
9	d	b	c	a
10	c	c	d	b
11	b	b	b	d
12	c	a	a	c
13	c	b	d	b
14	d	c	d	d
15	b	b	a	a
16	d	d	c	a
17	d	c	c	c
18	a	d	b	c
19	c	b	b	d
20	b	a	d	c
21	d	a	b	d
22	d	b	b	a
23	c	a	c	b
24	c	c	a	c
25	c	b	b	b
26	d	b	d	a
27	a	c	d	b
28	b	b	c	a
29	d	c	d	b
30	a	b	c	a
31	a	d	a	a
32	c	a	a	b
33	a	c	d	c
34	c	b	c	d
35	d	d	c	c
36	d	a	c	a
37	c	a	a	a
38	b	d	b	c
39	d	c	a	c
40	d	c	d	d
41	c	a	a	c
42	a	c	a	c
43	a	c	b	a